D1505006

Miranda Cosgrove

ABDO
Publishing Company

Big Buddy BOOKS
Buddy Bios

by Sarah Tieck

VISIT US AT
www.abdopublishing.com

Published by ABDO Publishing Company, 8000 West 78th Street, Edina, Minnesota 55439.

Printed in the United States of America, North Mankato, Minnesota.
112009
012010

 PRINTED ON RECYCLED PAPER

Coordinating Series Editor: Rochelle Baltzer
Contributing Editors: Heidi M.D. Elston, Megan M. Gunderson, BreAnn Rumsch, Marcia Zappa
Graphic Design: Maria Hosley
Cover Photograph: *AP Photo*: Chris Pizzello
Interior Photographs/Illustrations: *AP Photo*: Evan Agostini (p. 5), Mary Altaffer (p. 25), Lauren Greenfield/VII (pp. 20, 21), Curtis Means/NBC NewsWire via AP Images (p. 25), Charles Sykes (p. 27), Katy Winn/AP Images for Nickelodeon (p. 22); *Getty Images*: Frederick M. Brown (p. 9), Charley Gallay/WireImage (p. 25), Amy Graves/WireImage (p. 29), Scott Gries/Getty Images for Nickelodeon (p. 7), Mark Mainz (p. 15), Michael Rozman/FilmMagic.com (p. 11), John Shearer/WireImage (p. 19), Matthew Simmons (p. 17), Donald Weber (p. 12); *iStockphoto.com*: ©iStockphoto.com/ekash (p. 8).

Library of Congress Cataloging-in-Publication Data

Tieck, Sarah, 1976-
 Miranda Cosgrove : famous actress & singer / Sarah Tieck.
   p. cm. -- (Big buddy biographies)
 ISBN 978-1-60453-970-7
 1. Cosgrove, Miranda, 1993---Juvenile literature. 2. Actors--United States--Biography--Juvenile literature. 3. Singers--United States--Biography--Juvenile literature. I. Title.
 PN2287.C634T54 2010
 791.4302'8092--dc22
 [B]
                        2009032377

Miranda
Cosgrove

Contents

Rising Star

Miranda Cosgrove is a talented actress and singer. She has appeared in television shows and movies. Miranda is known for starring in the television show *iCarly*. She has also released popular music.

Miranda plays Carly Shay in *iCarly*.

5

Oregon

N
W   E
S

California   Nevada

PACIFIC OCEAN

Arizona

Los Angeles

MEXICO

Family Ties

Miranda Taylor Cosgrove was born in Los Angeles, California, on May 14, 1993. Her parents are Tom and Chris Cosgrove. Miranda has no brothers or sisters.

Sometimes, Miranda's mom attends events with her. She is one of Miranda's role models.

Growing Up

Miranda grew up in Los Angeles. There, her mother was a homemaker. Her father owned a dry-cleaning business.

Miranda attended Maude Price Elementary School in nearby Downey, California. Later, she was homeschooled. She learned from private teachers and on computers. This made it easier for Miranda to become a **professional** actress.

Miranda grew up in an ideal place to seek an acting career. Los Angeles is known for its acting opportunities.

Miranda's family has always supported her interest in music and acting.

9

Discovered!

Miranda was just three years old when she became a **professional** actress. She was discovered while dancing in a restaurant called Taste of LA. Soon after, she began appearing in television **commercials**.

Miranda is known for being very friendly with fans. She often signs autographs for them.

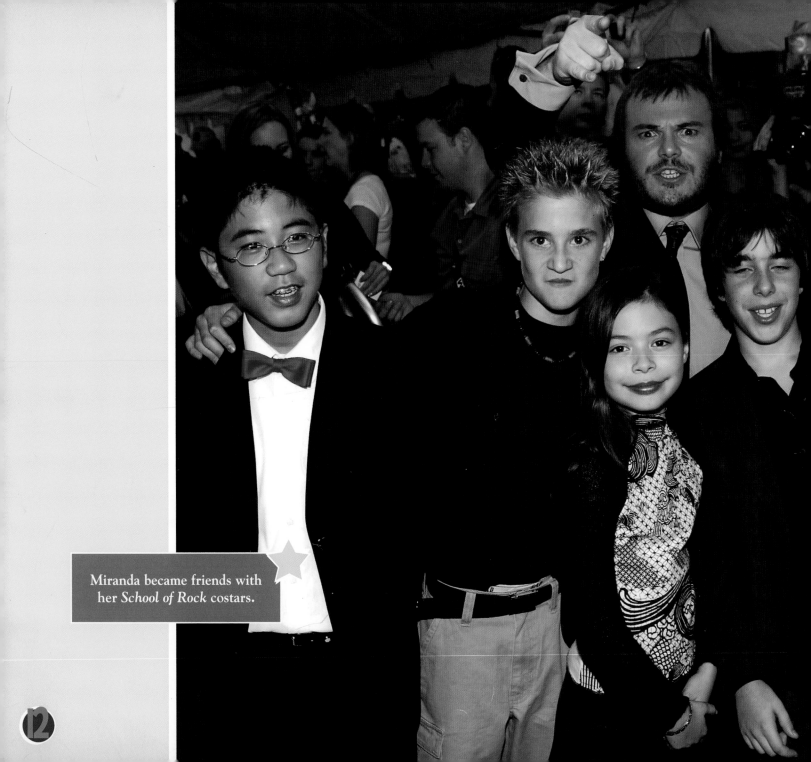

Miranda became friends with her *School of Rock* costars.

A Young Actress

Miranda wanted to act in television and movies. So, she **auditioned** for **roles**. In 2001, she got her first role! It was a small part on the television show *Smallville*.

In 2003, Miranda acted in her first movie. She played Summer Hathaway in the **comedy** *School of Rock*.

Miranda continued acting in movies. In 2005, she was in *Yours, Mine, and Ours*. The next year, Miranda acted in *Keeping Up with the Steins*. Both movies are **comedies**.

As an actress, Miranda often attends movie premieres.

Did you know...

Miranda played Drake's sister in *Yours, Mine, and Ours*. And later, Drake sang in Miranda's 2008 music video "Leave It All to Me."

Lights! Camera! Action!

In 2004, Miranda began appearing regularly on the television show *Drake & Josh*. The **comedy** follows the lives of teenage stepbrothers.

Miranda played Drake's little sister, Megan. On the show, Megan is often mean to her brothers.

Miranda became friends with *Drake & Josh* stars Drake Bell (*left*) and Josh Peck (*right*).

The cast of *Drake & Josh* filmed from about 2004 to 2007. The show was very popular on the Nickelodeon channel. It even won awards!

Miranda's work on *Drake & Josh* led to more opportunities. People liked her acting so much that she was given her own show!

Drake & Josh won Nickelodeon Kids' Choice Awards. It was named best TV show in 2006 and 2008.

Big Break

In 2007, Miranda began starring in *iCarly*. This was an important step in her acting **career**. Miranda played Carly Shay, a girl who has her own Web show with her friends.

After its **debut**, *iCarly* became one of Nickelodeon's most popular shows. Soon, a television movie was made. In 2008, Miranda starred in *iCarly: iGo to Japan*.

Jerry Trainor plays Carly's brother, Spencer, on *iCarly*.

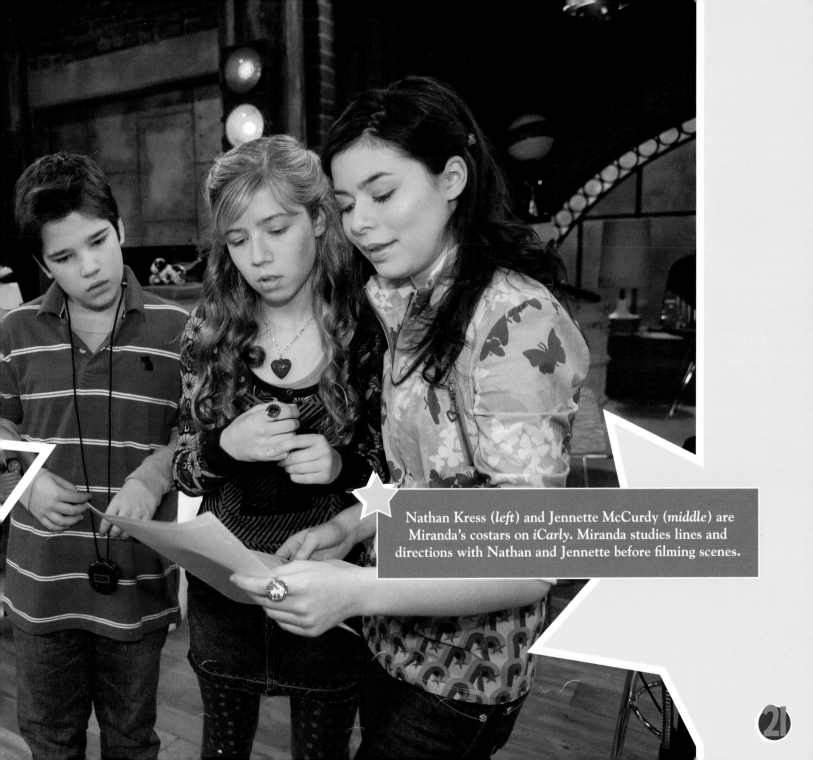

Nathan Kress (*left*) and Jennette McCurdy (*middle*) are Miranda's costars on *iCarly*. Miranda studies lines and directions with Nathan and Jennette before filming scenes.

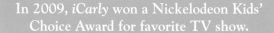

In 2009, *iCarly* won a Nickelodeon Kids' Choice Award for favorite TV show.

Did you know...

Miranda was nominated for several Young Artist Awards. She was named a possible winner for *Drake & Josh*, *Yours, Mine, and Ours*, and *School of Rock*. In 2009, Miranda won the award for her work on *iCarly*.

iCarly is known for its Web site. It has *iCarly* Web shows, just like the ones Carly and her friends make on the television show. These short shows only appear on the *iCarly* Web site. Sometimes fans send in their own Web videos, too.

Singing Sensation

In addition to her acting work, Miranda is a talented singer. She recorded the *iCarly* **theme song**, "Leave It All to Me." In 2008, it was **released** with other music on an album called *iCarly*.

In February 2009, Miranda released her first **solo** album. It is called *About You Now*.

Miranda performed "About You Now" in the 2008 Macy's Thanksgiving Day Parade.

The *iCarly* album featured Miranda's own music. It also included songs that the *iCarly* characters would enjoy.

Miranda got a guitar for her sixteenth birthday.

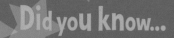

Off the Screen

When Miranda is not working, she hangs out with friends and family. She enjoys watching movies, driving, and playing tennis.

Miranda also likes riding horses. And, she has learned fencing. Fencing is a sport where people fight with special swords.

Miranda enjoys helping others. Sometimes she visits bookstores and reads to children.

Miranda has many fans. They often wait in long lines to meet her.

Buzz

Miranda's fame continues to grow. In 2009, she appeared in the movie *The Wild Stallion*. She also began work on the movie *Despicable Me*. And, she's helping to write songs for a new album.

Fans are excited to see what's next for Miranda Cosgrove. Many believe she has a bright **future**!

Snapshot

⭐**Name**: Miranda Taylor Cosgrove

⭐**Birthday**: May 14, 1993

⭐**Birthplace**: Los Angeles, California

⭐**Appearances**: *Smallville, School of Rock, Drake & Josh, Yours, Mine, and Ours, Keeping Up with the Steins, iCarly, iCarly: iGo to Japan, The Wild Stallion, Despicable Me*

⭐**Albums**: *iCarly, About You Now*

Important Words

audition (aw-DIH-shuhn) to give a trial performance showcasing personal talent as a musician, a singer, a dancer, or an actor.

career work a person does to earn money for a living.

comedy a funny story.

commercial (kuh-MUHR-shuhl) a short message on television or radio that helps sell a product.

debut (DAY-byoo) a first appearance.

future (FYOO-chuhr) a time that has not yet occurred.

professional (pruh-FEHSH-nuhl) working for money rather than for pleasure.

release to make available to the public.

role a part an actor plays.

solo a performance by a single person.

theme song the main tune or song from a movie or a television show.

Web Sites

To learn more about Miranda Cosgrove, visit ABDO Publishing Company online. Web sites about Miranda Cosgrove are featured on our Book Links page. These links are routinely monitored and updated to provide the most current information available.

www.abdopublishing.com

31

Index